Totally Gross & Awesome™
The Mayflower
Facts & Jokes

Published in MMXIX by
Scribo, an imprint of
The Salariya Book Company Ltd
25 Marlborough Place, Brighton BN1 1UB
www.salariya.com

ISBN: 978-1-912904-58-7

SALARIYA
SCRIBO BOOK HOUSE SCRIBBLERS

1 3 5 7 9 8 6 4 2

A CIP catalogue record for this book is available
from the British Library.

Printed and bound in China.
Printed on paper from sustainable sources.

Created and designed by
David Salariya.

Visit
www.salariya.com
for our online catalogue and
free fun stuff.

PAPER FROM

SUSTAINABLE
FORESTS

Author:
John Townsend worked as a high-
school teacher before becoming
a full-time writer. He specializes
in illuminating and humorous
information books for all ages.

Artist:
David Antram studied at
Eastbourne College of Art and then
worked in advertizing for 15 years
before becoming a full-time artist.
He has illustrated many children's
nonfiction books.

Totally Gross & Awesome™
The Mayflower Facts & Jokes

This Totally Gross & Awesome
book belongs to:

....

Written by
John Townsend

Illustrated by
David Antram

SCRIBO
a SALARIYA imprint

Introduction

We were so important in the making of modern America.

Warning—reading this book might not make you LOL (laugh out loud), but it could make you GOL (groan out loud), feel sick out loud, or SEL (scream even louder). If you are reading this in a library by a SILENCE sign... get ready to be thrown out!

Disclaimer: the author really hasn't made anything up in this book (apart from some daft limericks and jokes).

He checked out the foul facts as best he could and even double-checked the fouler bits to make sure, so please don't get too upset if you find out something different from a 17th century Native American, a Pilgrim leaping off a ship, or a stuffed Thanksgiving turkey.

If I had my way, I'd RATify everything!

Official

Warning

With the 400th Anniversary in 2020 of the sailing of the *Mayflower*, many Americans (especially in New England) wonder if they descended from those first Pilgrim Fathers who arrived in Cape Cod Bay in 1620. History books have long told of those brave pioneers of faith and courage who sailed to start a new great nation. However, there was more to it than that and it wasn't all plain sailing (very rough sailing, in fact). Before long, things turned nasty, with plenty of gruesome goings-on (and not just for turkeys).

So if my math is right, the first American Thanksgiving was in 1621.

In memory of Cape Cod, this year I've cooked cod with its eyes still in.

At least it should see us through the week.

The 400th anniversary of the first recorded American Thanksgiving feast in 2021 isn't much of a celebration if you're a turkey. They've been on the menu probably since that first feast, when other wildfowl, swan, and even eagle were dished up. Be prepared for more fowl and revolting details as we now set sail on a creaky old ship into choppy waters. You have been warned...

Loopy Limerick

In this totally gross and awesome book
Get ready to take a quick look
At history a-plenty
From the year sixteen twenty
And a boatload of gobbledegook...

As a Pilgrim, I object to all this twaddle.

What Is A Pilgrim?

A pilgrim is someone who makes a special journey, often a difficult one, to a distant place for religious reasons. (No, that doesn't mean a tourist to Disneyland at Christmas.)

It's so awesome being a devoted pilgrim.

Honey, you're a day-tripper on vacation and it's costing me a fortune.

Silly Verse

We came in the ship called
the Mayflower,
We're Pilgrims*—some say
that we're quirky...
But we're tough, with
unshakeable staying-power
And a taste for American turkey.

The Mayflower
was a ship called a
carrack, with 3 masts.

10

We've been squabbling about religion for centuries.

*The first Pilgrims were keen to start a new life with freedom from the rules of the Church of England. Puritans were another English religious group in the 16th and 17th centuries who disapproved of the Church of England and Roman Catholics. They wanted to make worship simpler and insisted on living lives of self-control. In fact, the Pilgrim Fathers weren't strictly Puritans but "separatists" who wanted to break away from the Church of England. Most Puritans who emigrated to North America came after 1630 in a time known as the Great Migration.

Lovely Leftovers

Did you know there's a sandwich named after some of the early settlers in America? A pilgrim or puritan is a popular snack attributed to the Pilgrim Fathers and the first Thanksgiving Day. Apparently, a traditional way of using leftover food from Thanksgiving Day was to put it between bread slices: layers of roast turkey, cranberries, and cheddar cheese.

Yes, even though no cows traveled on the *Mayflower*, it wasn't long before dairy cattle were introduced to America from England. Two Devon heifers and a bull were imported to the Plymouth colony in 1623. American cheddar cheese was soon on the menu along with all that wild turkey from the woods of New England.

I've had lots of calves so I must be a Pilgrim Mother.

Q: How did the Pilgrims take their cows to America?
A: On the Mooooo-flower.

Groan

Q: Why didn't the Puritans ever talk to turkeys?
A: They were easily offended by fowl language.

Q: Where did the
   Pilgrims stand
   when the *Mayflower*
   landed?
A: On their feet.

Reality Check

So what's all the fuss about this *Mayflower* business? What's the big deal? Time for the basics...

Before the year 1600, North America was fairly quiet with very few people living there, other than pockets of native Americans (later called "American Indians" by some Europeans). Meanwhile, Europe was packed with people in many large, ancient cities. In Britain, Queen Elizabeth I died and there were yet more arguments about how the country should be run, and especially about religion. Catholics and Protestants kept squabbling, but so did Protestants and Protestants. Some Protestants got so fed-up and worried they might get in trouble for disagreeing with everyone, that they were desperate to head off to somewhere new to start afresh. Along came a cunning plan...

16

In 1608, a group of English "separatists" escaped religious persecution by moving to Holland, where their ideas would be tolerated. Dutch people welcomed the Pilgrims, as they had come to be known. Even so, the Pilgrims found it hard to settle and decided to head off to somewhere new—where they could organize things just as they wanted. Somewhere across the world without many people seemed a good idea. The plan was to set sail across the Atlantic Ocean (almost 3,000 miles) in a ship called the *Mayflower* in 1620.

As queen, I was always arguing about religion and getting rid of anyone who disagreed with me.

Fast Facts

That Many People Don't Know...

 The *Mayflower* was not the first ship of British people to emigrate to America. Others had gone several years before.

2 The *Mayflower* set sail from Plymouth in Devon—correct? Not exactly. It first set off from London, then to Southampton, before loading up at Plymouth and heading off to America.

The *Mayflower* wasn't due to sail
alone. The Pilgrims hired a ship called
the *Speedwell* to take them from the
Netherlands to Southampton to meet up
with the *Mayflower*. The two ships were
to sail together to Northern Virginia,
but the journey got off to a bad start.
The *Speedwell* started leaking and had to
wait for repairs at Southampton.
Both ships finally set sail from Plymouth in
July, but about **300** miles (**483** kilometres)
from Lands End in Cornwall, western
England, they had to return to Devon to
leave the still leaky *Speedwell* behind.

Some of the Pilgrims saw this as a bad sign and gave up their plans to emigrate, while the rest boarded the *Mayflower* instead, which finally sailed off on September 6th 1620. Oops—being that late meant scary autumn storms were just ahead.

It's enough to make my heart sink—and everything else.

WHAT IF?
Limerick

If the Mayflower had never set sail,
Would the separatists end up in jail?
With no Mayflower ship
Meaning no Pilgrim trip
Could they worship or just weep and wail?

Meanwhile—on board ship as it's about to set sail, the captain was having a chat...

Susanna: Why is this ship called the *Mayflower*, Captain Jones?

Captain: No idea. If I had my way, it would be called Running Late.

Susanna: Why's that, captain?

Captain: Because, it's already September and May was four months ago.

Susanna: Do you feel like a game of cards?

Captain: Not now, if you don't mind. I'm happy just sitting on the deck.

Susanna: Why is it called the poop deck?

Captain: Have you seen all those seagulls?

Susanna: Captain, why don't you get measured for
           a new hat?

Captain: Not likely, I don't want to think about
          cap-sizing before we set off.

Susanna: Did you see how fast my husband rowed
           the paddles in our rowboat?

Captain: Yes, it was oar-inspiring.

Susanna: I insisted on him blowing up balloons and tying them under the hull.

Captain: Whatever floats your boat…

Susanna: There was a special offer on rowing paddles, so we bought hundreds.

Captain: That's quite an oar deal.

Susanna: I hope this ship is safe. I heard that two ships collided last week.

Captain: True. One was full of red paint and the other full of blue paint.

Susanna: I heard both their crews were marooned.

Captain: By the way, I want you to be in charge of the anchor.

Susanna: Why's that, Captain?

Captain: Because you keep sniffing and we need an anchor chief.

Susanna: Shall I weigh anchor right now?

They look like rats deserting a sinking ship.

Captain: There's no need—I know how heavy it is.

Susanna: I'm so excited to be one of your crew.

Captain: This journey will go down in history as the greatest voyage of all time.

Susanna: I used to think about time travel every day but that's now in the past.

Captain: I was going to tell you a joke about time travel but you didn't laugh.

Susanna: I'd love to be a time traveler. Unfortunately there's no future in it.

Captain: Doh!

For The Record

Susanna White was one of the pilgrims who achieved a number of "firsts." She survived the dangerous journey across the Atlantic despite being over six months pregnant. She gave birth to the first surviving baby in the new colony (while the ship was still in Cape Cod Bay). She called him Peregrine. She was apparently the first person to say on arriving at Plymouth Rock, "That's it?" Susanna also became the first bride in the new colony (just a few months after her first husband died). 1620 was quite a year for Susanna.

Peregrine means "one who journeys to foreign lands."

A Boatload of Random Facts

1 Essex was the English home county of many Pilgrims. John Carver of Braintree hired the *Mayflower*, Christopher Jones of Harwich was captain, and Samuel Fuller from Ockendon was ship's doctor. At least five of the passengers came from Billericay, including the treasurer, Christopher Martin. The town of Billerica, Massachusetts, was established in 1655 to commemorate the Essex home of those first settlers.

Seasickness keeps coming over me in huge waves.

2 About 20–30 men made up Captain Jones's crew on the ship. Not all the sailors and Pilgrims got on well. One of the sailors made fun of the seasick passengers and then he died suddenly. The Pilgrims said it was punishment from God.

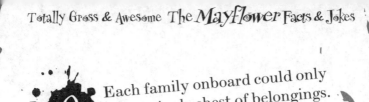

3 Each family onboard could only take a single chest of belongings. The entire journey took 66 days—just over two months.

4 At least one passenger, John Howland, was nearly killed when a storm almost swept him overboard. He was just able to grab hold of a rope and be pulled back aboard.

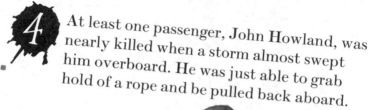

Yeeoow

5 Salty seawater was used for washing—but just a quick rinse rather than a proper bath. Yes, it got smelly, especially as no one could wash their clothes properly, which they wore for the whole journey (and probably slept in, too). Phewee.

6 Although there was a kitchen on the ship, most of the food would be dried or salted to stop it rotting. Most meals would be much the same, such as oatmeal, ship's biscuits, salted pork, cheese, beans, and fish. To wash that down, the pilgrims drank beer— including the thirty or so children on board. Beer was safer to drink than the risky water. They ate hardly any fruit or vegetables. Result = chronic constipation and illness from lack of vitamins. (No "five-a-day"—not even "one-a-day.")

7 The *Mayflower's* course was plotted by the captain using the stars. That took some skill as no GPS was available.

8 A baby boy, named Oceanus, was born while the *Mayflower* was on the way to North America. He later died at the age of two.

You've had the best berth on the ship.

A few children onboard were servants. Even though many Pilgrims thought their daughters were too weak to survive the hardships of the voyage, eleven girls made the trip, ranging in ages from 1 to 17 years old. Amazingly, only one young passenger (William Butten) died during the voyage. He came as a servant with the family of doctor Samuel Fuller. His master was sadly unable to help him as William was ill for much of the voyage and died just three days before land was sighted.

The Pilgrims were hoping to land in Virginia to make their new home. The King of England had given them permission to settle around the Hudson River (in what is now the state of New York). The perilous journey and running out of supplies threw the weary sailors a bit off course, so they sailed into Cape Cod Bay, without ever making it as far as Virginia.

Gross Alert

(not for the squeamish)

102 Pilgrims journeyed from England to the New World on the creaky ship, as well as cats, dogs, sheep, chickens, goats, and quite a few rats. Imagine the smell of being cooped up with that bunch for over two months, while people were being seasick. Poop buckets rolled across the decks during storms and bedding got drenched with unmentionables. The Pilgrims spent most of their time crammed below decks where they ate, slept on the floor, and used buckets or chamber pots. There were no windows in this area and it was often cold, damp, very dark, and always smelly. Oh yes, and there was always the fear that the ship could sink in a storm and you'd drown. Otherwise, it was probably quite nice.

Cape Cod

Fearing the ship would be destroyed in dangerous seas, the pilgrims sheltered inside Cape Cod Bay in the early morning of November 11, 1620 and anchored in what is now Provincetown Harbor. The men spent several weeks exploring Cape Cod, trying to decide where to build their homes before sailing across the bay to settle on the mainland...

We need a higher roof so let's have a party...

36

The women and children stayed on the *Mayflower*, wondering when or if the men would return. After two months, they finally found a place to settle. The harsh winter claimed many lives while the men built storehouses and living quarters. Finally, in March 1621, there were enough houses for everyone to live on land. At last the *Mayflower* left to return to England on April 5, 1621.

I'm happy to spend a night on the tiles.

And I'll sing loud enough to raise the roof.

3 Cape Cod Puns

Have you heard about the Cape Cod restaurant that caters just to dolphins? It only has one customer, but at least it serves a porpoise.

How do I decide on the worst joke? I'll flipper coin.

Why did the Cape Cod algae and the fungus get married? They took a lichen to each other (although, unfortunately, their marriage is now on the rocks).

Why did every Pilgrim climb off the *Mayflower* on to a rickety platform built by the crew, even though the posts in the water were giving way and they were scared? Pier pressure.

Loopy Limerick

As they clambered ashore at Cape Cod
Onto soil where none had yet trod
(so they thought),
The Pilgrims were shaken
By the sizzling of bacon...
"It's a barbecue—now that's
very odd!"
(Yes, the natives' campfires
weren't far away.)

Foul Weather & Fouler Times

Although the land was deserted, a few native American tribes lived nearby, so an exploring party with muskets was led by a soldier named Captain Miles Standish. Meanwhile, many of the women died from the bitter cold and diseases through the harsh winter.

My backside is colder than an ice bucket on the shady side of an iceberg.

41

It was tough work building their new colony (called Plymouth after the port of Plymouth they had sailed from in England). Their "Plymouth Plantation" was on the ruins of the native village of Pawtuxet.

The Pilgrims survived by stealing the food stores of neighboring native summer villages, as well as eating corn that was still growing wild from abandoned cornfields near the ruined village. The Pilgrims wrote a document called the Mayflower Compact setting down rules for living in their new community. That community had quite a few interesting characters. Meet them over the page...

It's colder than a rat catcher's heart.

43

Meet Six of The Cast...

1 Francis Billington

While the *Mayflower* was in Cape Cod Bay, teen Francis Billington was a bit of a wise guy. He and a friend got hold of his father's musket and fired it, showering sparks near an open barrel of gunpowder. It very nearly blew up the ship—which would have changed the course of history. After they'd settled ashore, members of Francis Billington's family were found guilty of all kinds of crimes, including murder. They were obviously the family you didn't want next door in a nice new colony!

> I always said those Billingtons were good for nothing rascals.

Mary Brewster

Mary Brewster was the wife of the Pilgrims' religious leader, William Brewster. She was obviously a tough cookie as she was one of only five adult women to survive the first winter at Plymouth and make it to the first Thanksgiving.

 ## Isaac Allerton

Isaac Allerton was something of a "wheeler-dealer" and was among the pilgrims responsible for repaying the people back home who'd paid for their voyage. But instead, he helped himself to the funds and was banished from the colony. Somehow he survived and did well for himself—ending up with houses in both New Haven and Lower Manhattan, near where Wall Street stands today. Enough said.

4 Stephen Hopkins

The *Mayflower* voyage was Stephen Hopkins's second trip to the New World. His first was to Jamestown, Virginia, but that ship was wrecked off Bermuda (maybe the Bermuda Triangle was scary even then). There Hopkins narrowly escaped being hanged for causing trouble. He eventually returned to England, only to come back aboard the *Mayflower*. In Plymouth, he set up the first tavern, where he was fined several times for serving alcohol on a Sunday (not allowed in the Mayflower Compact). Yet again, this colorful character was getting into all kinds of trouble and being punished for breaking the rules. He certainly wasn't a Puritan.

The rule to ban drinking was met by a chorus of booze (boos).

Edward Doty and Edward Leister

Edward Doty and Edward Leister were servants of Stephen Hopkins. No one knows why these two Eds got into a blazing argument and fought the first duel in the New World. Their punishment was to be tied together hand and foot for 24 hours. Doty spent the rest of his life in Plymouth, where he was infamous for his terrible temper. He appeared in court various times but seemed to get away with avoiding serious punishment.

Alice Mullins

6 Alice Mullins was married to shoemaker William Mullins, who brought 250 shoes and 13 pairs of boots with him on the *Mayflower*. But, although never short of shoes to wear, Alice died soon after arriving at Plymouth. Even so, she left many descendants, one of whom was the famous film star Marilyn Monroe, who also had plenty of fancy shoes, to boot (as it were).

I had to burn Alice's shoes. It was sole destroying.

At Church One Sunday

(Can you find the BIG mistake hiding in the pews?)

William Brewster: Fellow Pilgrims, we are gathered here in church this Sunday...

Mary Brewster: Sorry, sir—I can't stay as I've got to cook lunch. *(dashes off)*

William: After all our trials, Pilgrims, at last we have found peace and happiness...

Francis: What happens if I pull this trigger... *BANG.* Oops. *(dashes off)*

William: Can someone send for Doctor Fuller? It looks like Francis has shot one of the congregation. Meanwhile we'll pass around the money plate and take the collection…

Isaac Allerton: I'll happily take the collection for you… *(grabs it and dashes off)*

You see, not all Pilgrims were holy, honest, and decent. Far from it!

Stephen Hopkins: Hey, that's against the rules of the Mayflower Compact. Anyway, what do I care—I've got to go and serve drinks in my pub… *(dashes off)*

Alice Mullins: Sorry, Mr. Brewster—I've got to go, too. I've come in the wrong shoes and in this snow I might catch my death… *(dashes off)*

William: Will you please all stand as we sing the hymn:

> *"Then fancies fly away,*
> *we'll fear not*
> *what men say,*
> *We'll labor night and day—*
> *to be a pilgrim."*

Edward Doty: I'm not singing this—I'm not going to labor night and day for anyone.

Edward Leister: You've never lifted a finger. I have to do all the work.

Edward Doty: Right, that's it. I challenge you to a duel.

Edward Leister: You'll have to catch me first. *(dashes off)*

Edward Doty: That's just what I'm gonna do. I can beat you by miles... *(dashes off)*

Miles Standish: Don't drag me into this—but I'll soon sort you two out... *(dashes off)*

William: Dearly beloved, we are gathered here... Oh, it looks like it's just me left. Do you know, sometimes I wonder why we bothered. *(dashes off)*

I spotted the mistake. That hymn is from John Bunyan's *The Pilgrim's Progress*, written 50 years later.

Silly Riddles

Q: How did the *Mayflower* show that it loved America?
A: It hugged the shore for days.

It's so grisly here—can you bear a hug?

Q: If the Pilgrims were still alive today, what would they be famous for?
A: Their age.

Q: If April showers bring May flowers, what do May flowers bring?
A: Pilgrims.

William Bradford

We wouldn't know much about the Pilgrims arriving at Cape Cod if it weren't for one of them writing a journal. He was William Bradford, an orphan from Yorkshire. He eventually became governor in the new colony for over thirty years and wrote *Of Plymouth Plantation*, the first work of American history. This is how he told of arriving safely at Cape Cod:

"Being thus arrived in a good harbor and brought safe to land, they fell upon their knees and blessed God of heaven, who had brought them over the vast and furious ocean.

But they had now no friends to welcome them, nor inns to entertain or refresh their weather-beaten bodies, no houses or much less towns to repair to.

Ought not the children of these pilgrim fathers rightly say: our fathers were Englishmen which came over this great ocean and were ready to perish in this wilderness; but they cried unto the Lord, and he heard their voice, and looked on their adversity." (paraphrased)

Look out—that kid's got a gun!

Just imagine if young rascal Francis Billington had written a blog:

I'm gonna tell it as it is. This place is real boring. It's a dump. There's nothing here. They call it Cape Cod but there are no beach chairs, no frisbees, no ice cream—nothing. The journey here was so gross.

That ship is one big heap of garbage—full of sick, poop, rats, pee, screaming kids, lice, fleas, maggots—and that's on a good day. They chewed my ear off when I let off dad's gun for a laugh. They went ballistic and told me off for trying to blow us up. I was doing us all a favor, I figure.

Don't pull the trigger!

Now we've landed at this slum, I hate it. There's just a dirty great lump of rock, emptiness, swamp, and absolutely no nightlife. Believe me, nothing will ever happen here. No one's ever gonna hear of America or us again. This place is so yesterday. *#get-me-outta-here*

You just can't please some kids these days.

Just when you thought you were getting the gist of all this Mayflower history, it's time to bust a few old myths...

We're about to scrape the bottom of the barrel.

Myth 1:

The Mayflower passengers always wore black without any color and had big buckles.

I'm not a myth— I'm a myth-ter and you're my mythuss.

Not so. Some Puritans later wore black and white, but not the original Pilgrims. When a *Mayflower* passenger died, a list of their belongings was published. John Howland had two red vests. William Bradford had a green gown, a violet cloak, a suit with silver buttons, and a red vest. William Brewster had green underwear, a red cap, and a violet coat. Children probably wore a lot of blues and yellows. And as for those tall hats with buckles that often appear in paintings… Historians tell us Pilgrims didn't have buckles on their clothing, shoes, or hats. Buckles did not come into fashion until the late 1600s—more likely at the time of the Salem Witchcraft trials in 1693, but that's quite another story!

So, this old joke doesn't actually make sense…

Q: Why did the Pilgrims pants keep falling down?
A: Because their belt buckles were on their hats.

Myth 2:

The Mayflower passengers were strict religious people who disapproved of fun, parties, and enjoying life.

Not so—as some of those passengers were more concerned about starting afresh and making a better, more enjoyable life for their families by starting businesses and trade. It wasn't so much religion that drove many of them, but rather new opportunities, better chances, and the hope of getting rich. Anyway, the Pilgrims must have liked loud music, bands, and screaming singers. After all, they were really into Plymouth Rock!

Myth 3:

Pilgrims lived in log cabins soon after they arrived.

Not so. The log cabin didn't appear in America until late in the seventeenth century, when it was introduced by Germans and Swedes. It seems the term "log cabin" isn't found in print before the 1770s. Log cabins were virtually unknown in England at the time the Pilgrims arrived in America. So what kind of dwellings did the Pilgrims build for themselves? True, they would have used timber, but not hefty great tree trunks, just sawn planks and boards—not a log in sight.

Tougher Times Ahead

By mid-1621, 46 of the original 102 *Mayflower* Pilgrims had died. It was local Native Americans who came to the rescue. Just imagine how surprised the Pilgrims were when a dark mysterious stranger turned up and spoke to them in English.

I say, how do you do, chaps?

It's terribly lovely to meet you.

A chief from an Abenaki tribe from what is today Maine was named Samoset. He had learned to speak English from fishermen who visited his camp. Fearing they were about to be attacked, the Pilgrims of Plymouth Plantation were shocked when he entered their settlement and announced, "Welcome, Englishmen!" Samoset was friendly and offered his help.
He introduced a friend of his named Squanto from the Wampanoag tribe. Amazingly, he spoke very good English because he'd been captured by the English in 1614 as a slave and taken to Spain, but later escaped.

I've got a fowl feeling this isn't going to go well.

Fishy or what?

Squanto, also known as Tisquantum, became a trusted interpreter and guide to the Pilgrim settlers at Plymouth. He taught them how to grow corn, to hunt, catch wild turkeys, and to enrich the soil by burying fish heads with the seeds (nothing like a bit of fish compost to feed the crop).

It seems some of the Wampanoag people (the original natives of Massachusetts and Rhode Island) thought there was something extra fishy going on and they captured Squanto after the first Thanksgiving celebrations. Miles Standish and other Pilgrims didn't want to lose their interpreter, so they promptly rescued him in a daring raid and brought him back.

Losing A Friend

We don't know much more about Squanto, but it seems he became ill with a fever in 1622. His nose began to bleed and he was dead in a few days. Some historians think he may have been poisoned by his own Wampanoag people. Unfortunately, the relationship between the British immigrants and the Wampanoag went from bad to worse, with diseases brought from England, as well as attacks wiping out most of the Wampanoag. Descendants of the surviving Wampanoag people are still living in New England today.

Did you hear the one about the Pilgrim and the bison?

A devout Pilgrim lost his Bible soon after staggering ashore from the *Mayflower*. Three weeks later, a bison walked up to him carrying the Bible in its mouth. The Pilgrim couldn't believe his eyes. He took the precious book out of the bison's mouth, raised his eyes heavenward, and exclaimed, "It's a miracle!"

"Not really," said the bison. "Your name is written inside the cover."
"Where did you find it?" the pilgrim asked.
"To be honest," the bison said, "I borrowed it from off your shelf. You could say it was a buffa-loan!"

Mooooo

The First Thanksgiving

Thanksgiving Day is now a BIG event, right? And it all started from the Pilgrim Fathers in their first year in America, right? Hmmm, this is where things get messy. Be prepared to be shocked, outraged, upset, horrified, or just bored to tears. Brace yourself for a few Thanksgiving MYTHS…

We Pilgrims believe in sharing everything.

Yeah – like sharing their diseases.

Myth 1:

The first Thanksgiving was in 1621 and the Pilgrims then celebrated it every year thereafter. Wrong.

The first feast wasn't repeated, so it wasn't the beginning of a tradition. In fact, the Pilgrims didn't even call the day Thanksgiving. It was just a harvest supper to bring the communities together. In 1621, the Plymouth colonists and Wampanoag neighbors shared an autumn harvest feast, which was probably one of the first Thanksgiving celebrations in the colonies. For more than two centuries, days of thanksgiving were celebrated by different colonies and states.

What a night for fireworks on the big 400th anniversary. Thursday, November 24, 2021 will long be remembered as 'Thanksgiving 400' (until the BIG 500th!)

Do you know when Thanksgiving Day is held each year?

Myth 2:

The original Thanksgiving feast took place on the fourth Thursday of November. Wrong.

The original feast in 1621 was sometime between September 21 and November 11. Unlike the modern holiday, it probably lasted about three days. The event was based on English harvest festivals, which traditionally occurred around September 29.

Myth 3:

The original Thanksgiving meal was roast turkey, cranberry sauce, and all the trimmings. Wrong.

The traditional Thanksgiving menu of turkey, stuffing, mashed potatoes, candied yams, cranberry sauce, and pumpkin pie wouldn't have been on the menu at that first Thanksgiving. Maybe wildfowl of some sort was there, corn, porridge, and venison. It's pretty certain any sort of pie was off the menu as butter and flour were very rare, as were proper ovens for baking them. No one would have eaten with a fork, either—as they didn't have forks back then. So Thanksgiving would have been finger-lickin' good.

81

Gross Alert

Sadly, the friendliness at that first Thanksgiving didn't last. As more European immigrants arrived (Puritans), there were many clashes with Native Americans. Look away now if you're squeamish…

By 1675, Massachusetts and surrounding colonies were at war with the Wampanoag people. The Wampanoag leader, named Metacomet, was angry at the destruction of his culture and his people. He was forced to strike out and raid settlers' homes. Captain Benjamin Church tracked down and killed Metacomet. His body was drawn and quartered, and his entrails were "left for the wolves." His head was sent to Plymouth where it was put up on a pole for all to see. The spirit of Thanksgiving soon turned very grim.

Tragically, the new settlers also brought the smallpox virus with them. Deadly breakouts plagued local tribes and killed an estimated 90% of native people in the New England area.

Quick History Lesson

The Thanksgiving holiday that most Americans celebrate each November has little to do with that first sharing of a meal between Pilgrims and Native Americans. It was during the American Revolution in 1777 when General George Washington asked for a day of prayer and thanksgiving. Not all states observed such a day.

No turkeys, no pumpkins, no wonder, November!

Many years later, it was President Abraham Lincoln who established a National Day of Thanksgiving in 1863. This was a plea to all Americans to have a day of prayer and thanksgiving during the Civil War—on Thursday, November 26.

The holiday has been proclaimed by every president since, with the date changing a few times until 1941 when Congress made the fourth Thursday of November a legal holiday for a National Day of Thanks.

There's always something to be thankful for on Thanksgiving. Apart from anything else, just give thanks you're not a turkey.

Please don't read this
bit if you're a turkey

Try these for some
Thanksgiving fowl figures

1 According to
people with super-
calculators and
nothing better to
do, Americans spend
something like
2½ billion dollars
at Thanksgiving
to stock up on
turkey, stuffing,
potatoes, and other
holiday goodies.

2 More than 50 million turkeys will be consumed on Thanksgiving alone (that's a lot of gobbling—about a fifth of the almost 250 million turkeys raised per year in America). Oh yes… and getting on for 50 million Americans will travel 50 miles (80 kilometres) or more for Thanksgiving dinner. Is Thanksgiving really good for the planet? (Don't even think about greenhouse gases and windy Black Friday).

Thanksgiving Hymn

May your stuffing be great
And your turkey be plumped,
May the pile on your plate
Never need stomachs pumped.
May your feast be a winner
And your pies take the prize,
May your Thanksgiving dinner
Not go straight to your thighs.

I just burned
up 10,000 calories.
The roast turkey
caught fire.

Daft Riddles

Q: What happened to the Pilgrim who was shot at by a Native American after the second Thanksgiving?

A: He had an arrow escape.

Q: How do you keep a
turkey in suspense?
A: I'll tell you later.

Q: How does Thanksgiving
usually start?
A: With a T.

Q: What always comes at
the end of Thanksgiving?
A: The letter G.

Q: No, really—what comes at the end of Thanksgiving?

I figure Black Friday is a mug's game.

Real Answer: The day after Thanksgiving has been called Black Friday since at least the early 1960s. The reason for the day's name is that it's apparently the first day of the year when stores are starting to make healthy profits, so they are in the black rather than being in the red. Hence all those crazy sales. It might have something to do with businesses trying to make people spend more in the period leading up to Christmas, too!

You Couldn't Make It Up

Of all those millions of turkeys killed for Thanksgiving celebrations, a couple get lucky. Every year the President is given a turkey to be officially "pardoned" and its life is spared. A second "fallback" turkey also escapes the chop. A total of eight birds are randomly chosen as they hatch, which are then narrowed down to the two largest and best-behaved birds. Both birds are then spared by the president. Survival of the fattest!

Get ready to shed a tear now...
The lucky pair live happily ever
after for the rest of their days in
Virginia at George Washington's
former estate, Mount Vernon.

I've got some good news and some bad news...

Turkey Trots

What about the tradition of cracking a turkey bone?

The wishbone was once a symbol of luck, and the tradition of breaking a turkey wishbone for Thanksgiving started with the Pilgrims, according to old legend (but more than likely it's a lot of turkey GOBBLEdegook). Yes, legend has it that if two people hold the wishbone, make a wish, and break it apart, the person holding the longer piece will have their wish granted. Maybe lucky for some—but not the turkey.

Some people aren't just happy to chomp turkey drumsticks at Thanksgiving. Over recent years, people across the country have taken to running around like turkeys. They take part in Turkey Trots, when they dress up as the birds and do fun runs or even marathons. Is there no end to this national obsession with upsetting turkeys?

What's the difference between chickens and turkeys?

Chickens celebrate Thanksgiving

Timeline

A final reminder about early America

1 **1000 CE**
Leif Ericson (a Viking explorer) discovers Vinland (probably Newfoundland, but possibly New England).

I bet this country won't come to much.

2 1492

Christopher Columbus discovers the New World.

3 1507

New World named after Americus Vespucius (a Spanish explorer born in Italy).

4 1524

Verrazano (Italian) and Gomez (Portuguese) explore New England's coast.

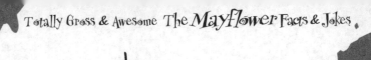

5 1579

Francis Drake of England explores the coast of California.

I name this place Virginia—for my Queen Elizabeth of England.

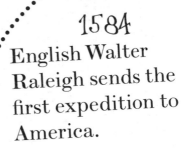

6 1584

English Walter Raleigh sends the first expedition to America.

7 1604

Acadia (northeast North America) is settled by the French.

98

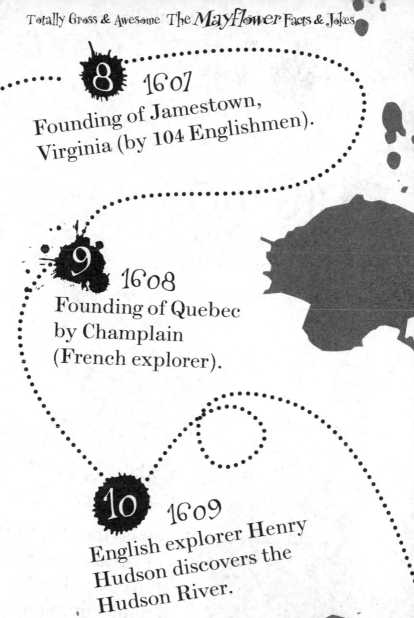

8 16·07
Founding of Jamestown, Virginia (by 104 Englishmen).

9 16·08
Founding of Quebec by Champlain (French explorer).

10 16·09
English explorer Henry Hudson discovers the Hudson River.

11

1619
The first African slaves are sold in Virginia.

12

1620
Arrival of the Pilgrims in the *Mayflower.*

13

1621
53 surviving Pilgrims celebrate their harvest: "First Thanksgiving in Plymouth."

14

1623

Settlements start at New Amsterdam.
First settlements in New Hampshire.

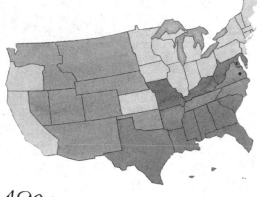

15

1630

The "Great Migration"
to Massachusetts. The
founding of Boston.

16

1637

War with Pequot Native
Americans. First African
slaves arrive in New England.

Just A Reminder

New England comprises the states of Maine, Vermont, New Hampshire, Massachusetts, Connecticut, and Rhode Island. All but two (Maine and Vermont) were among the thirteen former British colonies that became the United States in 1776. Many of the "original thirteen" had begun well over 100 years before, including the first colony of Virginia, which was founded in 1607.

But we were here long before!

New Hampshire

Vermont

Maine

Massachusetts

Rhode island

Connecticut

And Finally...

Mayflower 400—the Big Party of 2020.

"Mayflower 400 celebrates the values of freedom, faith, and personal liberty that informed the original journey, and which continue in the special relationship between the UK, US, and Netherlands. The commemorations recognize the impact of the *Mayflower*'s journey on Native American communities and address themes of colonialism and migration, providing inclusive accounts of the *Mayflower*'s legacy." (Thus says the Mayflower 400 organization.)

Can You Believe It?

Of the **102** *Mayflower* passengers, only **29** are known to have had descendants. But from that small number, it has been estimated that **35** million people worldwide, and **10** million in the United States, are descended today. Only about **25,000** people have been able to trace family histories back to those original voyagers. Quite a few famous people are counted among those descendants and hey, **YOU** could be too!

My family tree is a walnut— most of my ancestors were nuts.

105

Last Joke

The Taylor Family from Rhode
Island were very proud of
their heritage. Their ancestors
had traveled to America with
the Pilgrim Fathers on the
Mayflower. Those Pilgrims'
descendants included
Congressmen, successful
bankers, artists, famous sports
people, and Hollywood stars.

On the 400th Anniversary of the sailing of the *Mayflower*, young Trixie Taylor decided to research and write a family history, something to present one day for her children and grandchildren. She found a specialist historian to help look through all the archives. There was just one problem—how to mention Great Great Uncle Jefferson Lincoln Taylor, who was executed in the electric chair for his life of villainy and crime. Trixie said she could deal with their family's "skeleton in the cupboard" tactfully. When her family history was finally published, the short section about the notorious Jefferson read:

Great Great Uncle Jefferson Lincoln Taylor was well known by the civic authorities for his impact on the lives of many. He occupied a chair of applied electronics at an important government institution, where he was attached to his position by the strongest of ties. His death came as a great shock.

A Silly Play Skit

Pilgrim Father: Can you teach me how to hunt wild animals?

Native American: Sure. Would you like to hunt bear?

Pilgrim Father: Certainly not—I prefer to keep my clothes on at all times.

Native American: Ever seen a grizzly?

Pilgrim Father: Yes, my wife is always very grizzly and grumpy in the mornings. In fact, today she sprang out of bed and shot a chipmunk in her nightie.

Native American: Funny place to find a chipmunk.

Pilgrim Father: In fact, I found a skunk in my pants yesterday.

Native American: What about the foul smell?

Pilgrim Father: It didn't seem to mind. How about hunting buffalo?

Native American: It's bison around here.

Pilgrim Father: Really? What's the difference between a buffalo and a bison?

Native American: Have you ever tried to wash your hands in a buffalo? Bison can be dangerous, so always track them with care.

Pilgrim Father: You know how to follow bison tracks?

Native American: Bison leave many clues behind. Many from their behinds.

Pilgrim Father: What can you see under the feet of bison?

Native American: Squashed bison-hunters who are too slow. You Pilgrims must learn respect for bison. Once they came into camp and into our tepees.

Pilgrim Father: What's that like?

I ran into a tepee and a wigwam but freaked out. The atmosphere was just two tents.

Native American: Intense.

Pilgrim Father: In tents? They actually run through your wigwams?

Native American: No, they ran. Past tense.

Pilgrim Father: Past tents? In tents? I'm confused.

Native American: Bison slept under my bed last night.

Pilgrim Father: How did you know?

Native American: I woke up with my nose on the roof of the tepee.

Pilgrim Father: And I thought waking up with mice under my bed was bad enough.

Native American: Do you know how to tell the difference between having a mouse or a bison under the bed?

Pilgrim Father: How?

Native American: If you can't pick it up by the tail, it must be a bison. There again, it could be a very overweight mouse.

Pilgrim Father: Doh!

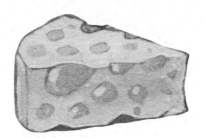

Final Teaser

If you survived some of the totally gross and awesome facts and jokes in this book, take a look at the other wacky titles in this revolting series. They're all guaranteed to make you groan and squirm like never before. Share them with your friends AT YOUR OWN RISK!

QUIZ

1. Where in America did the Mayflower arrive in 1620?

a) Cape Dolphin Cove

b) Cape Cod Bay

c) Long Island Sound

2. Why did the Pilgrim Fathers set sail on the Mayflower?

a) To start a new life together in the way they wanted.

b) To find gold and get rich.

c) To enjoy a warmer climate and better food.

3. Which English port did the Mayflower sail from?

a) Liverpool

b) Harwich

c) Plymouth

4. Who was the first baby to be born and survive in the New World?

a) Peregrine White

b) Archibald Black

c) Dorothy Gray

5. Where were the Pilgrim Fathers hoping to arrive in America?

a) Florida

b) California

c) Virginia

6. Why did more than 40 pilgrims die in the first months in America?

a) From cold and malnutrition.

b) From the plague.

c) From attacks by Native Americans.

7. How did Pilgrims and Wampanoag people celebrate together in 1621?

a) They shared a harvest supper.

b) They held the very first baseball game.

c) They cooked a massive barbecue with a spit-roasted bison.

8. Which holiday marks that first celebration?

a) Groundhog Day

b) Memorial Day

c) Thanksgiving Day

9. Which day follows the traditional turkey feast each year?

a) Red Tuesday

b) Black Friday

c) Blue Monday

10. What happened within a few years of the Mayflower's arrival in America?

a) The first Disney World opened.

b) New York City was built.

c) Many more Europeans settled along the east coast.

Answers:

1 = b
2 = a
3 = c
4 = a
5 = c
6 = a
7 = a
8 = c
9 = b
10 = c

GLOSSARY

Colony: a territory under the control of another nation or foreign settlers.

Compact: an official agreement.

Descendant: someone who is related to a person from a previous generation, such as a grandchild of a grandparent.

Emigrate: to leave a country or region to live elsewhere.

Protestant: a branch of the Christian church which was developed in the 16th century by Christians who disliked the Catholic Church.

Puritan: a member of the 16th- and 17th-century Protestants in England and New England who opposed many customs of the Church of England and preached stricter moral rules.

Wampanoag: Native Americans of Massachusetts and Eastern Rhode Island, who befriended settlers until most were killed in battles begun by colonists taking their land.

INDEX

Watch for other wacky books in this series... if you dare!

I finished reading this Totally Gross & Awesome book on:

........../........../..........